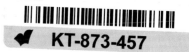

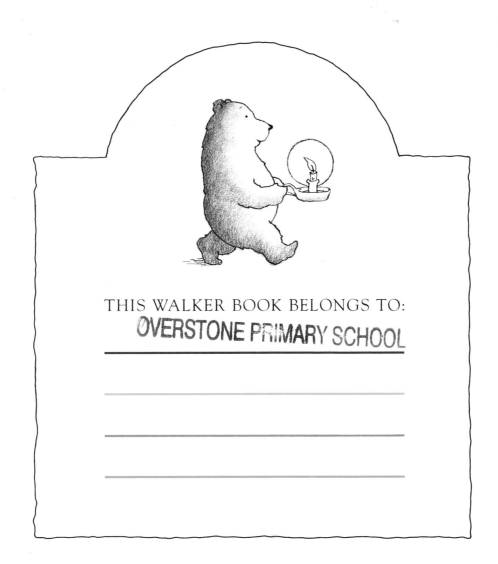

THIS WALKER BOOK BELONGS TO:

Limestone
Birdsmouth brick
Sandstone
Saddleback coping brick
Cownose brick
frog
header
bed
stretcher
The parts of a brick
Granite
Bullnose brick
Marble

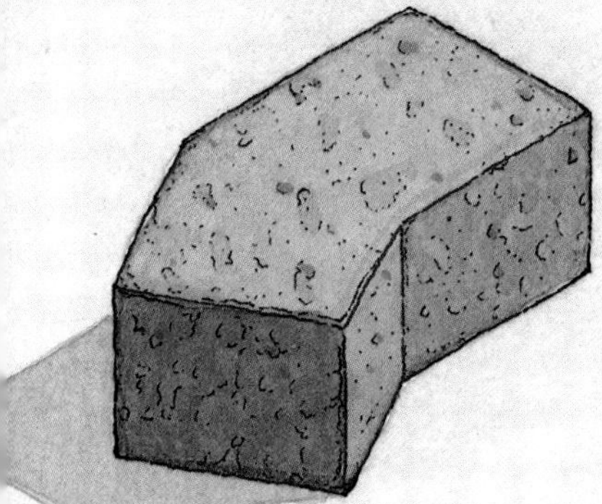

Dogleg brick

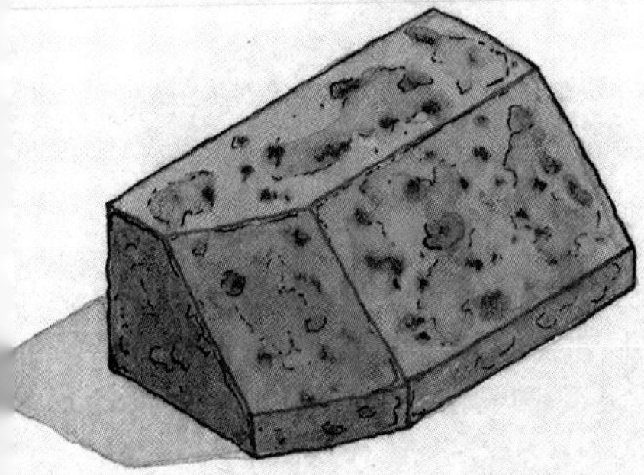

Plinth squint brick

Limestone sneck

You probably know that some walls are built of stone (which is natural) and some are built of bricks (which are man-made), but did you know that walls can be built of almost anything? Look inside to find out about walls made of rubber, wax, metal, glass, wood, ice, and alligators – and see if you can think of any other kinds.

Be careful about climbing on walls, though, whatever they're made of. Remember what happened to Humpty Dumpty!

Bevelled bat brick

Half round coping brick

Decorative brick

For Lucy and Emily

J.A.

For Amelia

A.B.

First published 1993
by Walker Books Ltd
87 Vauxhall Walk
London SE11 5HJ

This edition published 2001

2 4 6 8 10 9 7 5 3 1

This book has been typeset in Garamond Light

Printed in Hong Kong

British Library Cataloguing in Publication Data:
a catalogue record for this book is available
from the British Library

ISBN 0-7445-7895-7

WHAT IS A WALL AFTER ALL?

Judy Allen

illustrated by

Alan Baron

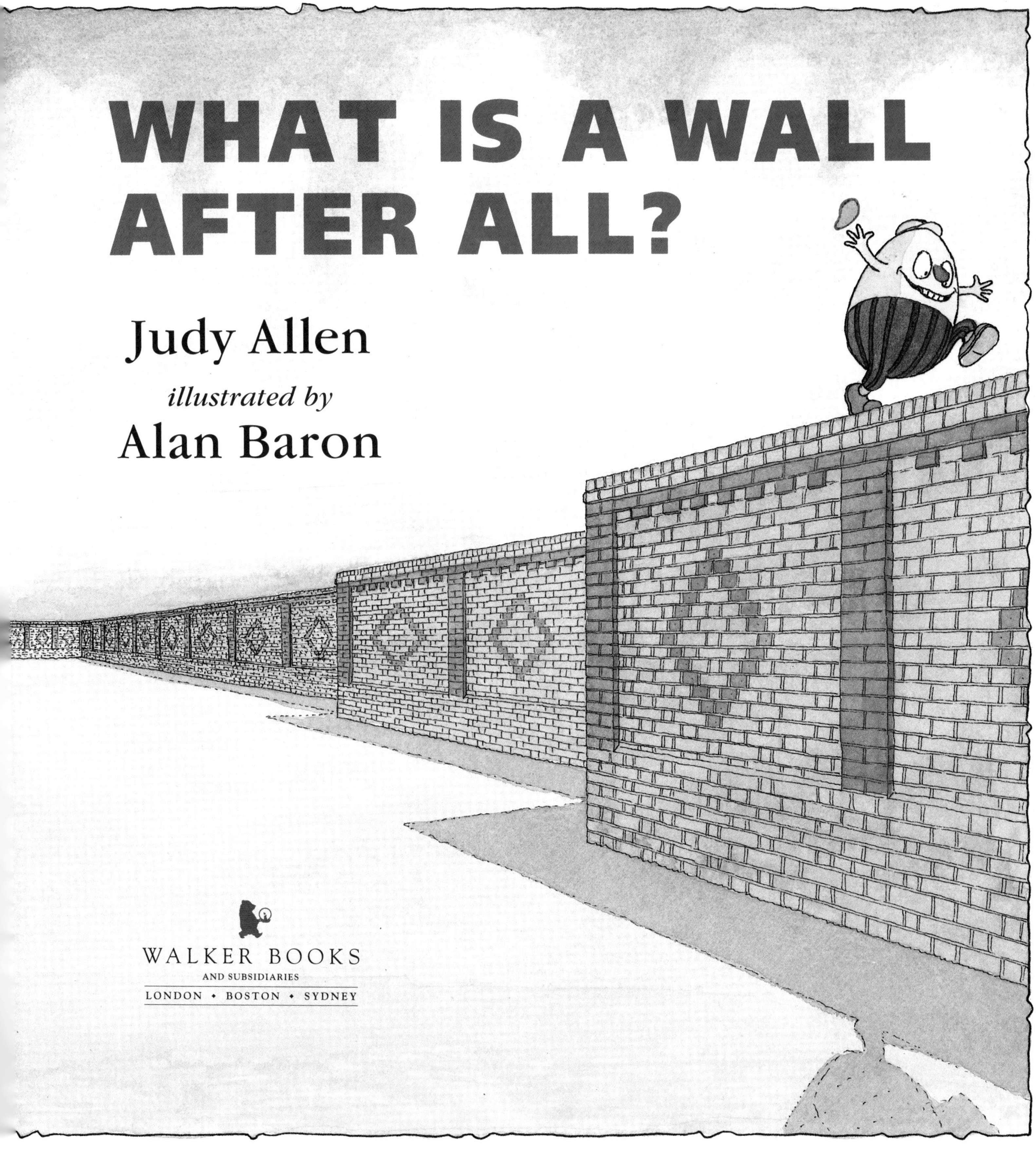

WALKER BOOKS
AND SUBSIDIARIES
LONDON • BOSTON • SYDNEY

Weather boards
Clinker blocks
PALLADIUM
WAS HUMPTY DUMPTY PUSHED?
You can build a wall of almost anything.
Even alligators?
Don't be silly. Whoever heard of a wall of alligators?

Wherever you are when you open this book,

Gable end
Cornerstones
Saddle-back Coping
Imagine if there were no walls...
What would hold the roofs up?
This beehive has walls made of wood!
The bees are building tiny wax walls inside it so they can store their honey.
They've been taking nectar from this wallflower.

I bet you can see a wall, if you look.

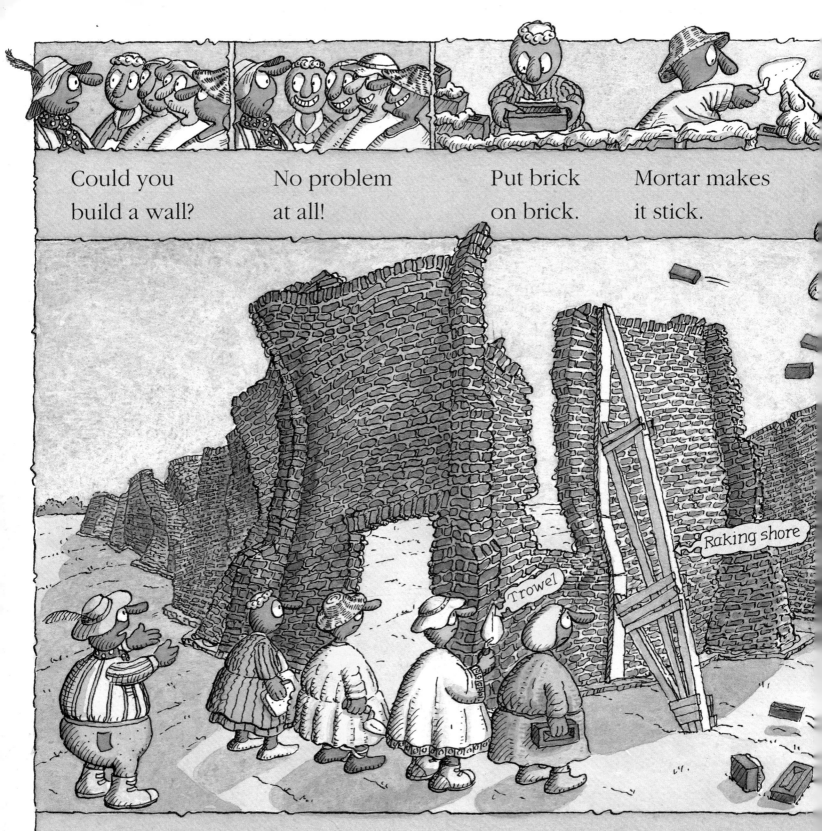

Could you build a wall?

No problem at all!

Put brick on brick.

Mortar makes it stick.

It's a weak wall, a sick wall, a leaning-on-a-stick wall,
a feeble wall, a quaky wall, a crumbly, tumbly, shaky wall.

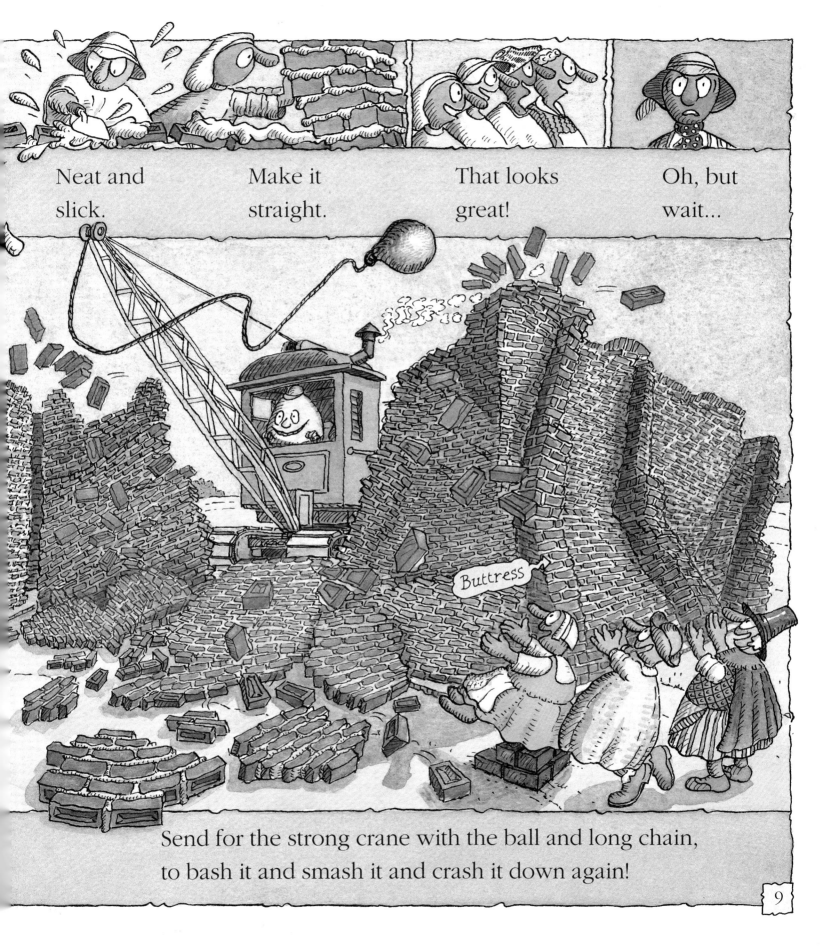

Neat and slick.

Make it straight.

That looks great!

Oh, but wait...

Send for the strong crane with the ball and long chain,
to bash it and smash it and crash it down again!

A drystone wall may look like a huddle
of jagged stones, ragged stones, all in a muddle,
a jumble that could easily tumble and fall.
Look carefully, though, it's cleverly done:
each stone is balanced on another one.
Each shape has been picked to fit its own space,
so the wall stands firm on a solid base.

Why is it called a drystone wall?
Because it doesn't have wet putty or mortar to hold it together.
If it rains, will it be a wetstone wall?
No! It'll be a wet drystone wall.
Copestone
Throughstone
Foundation stone

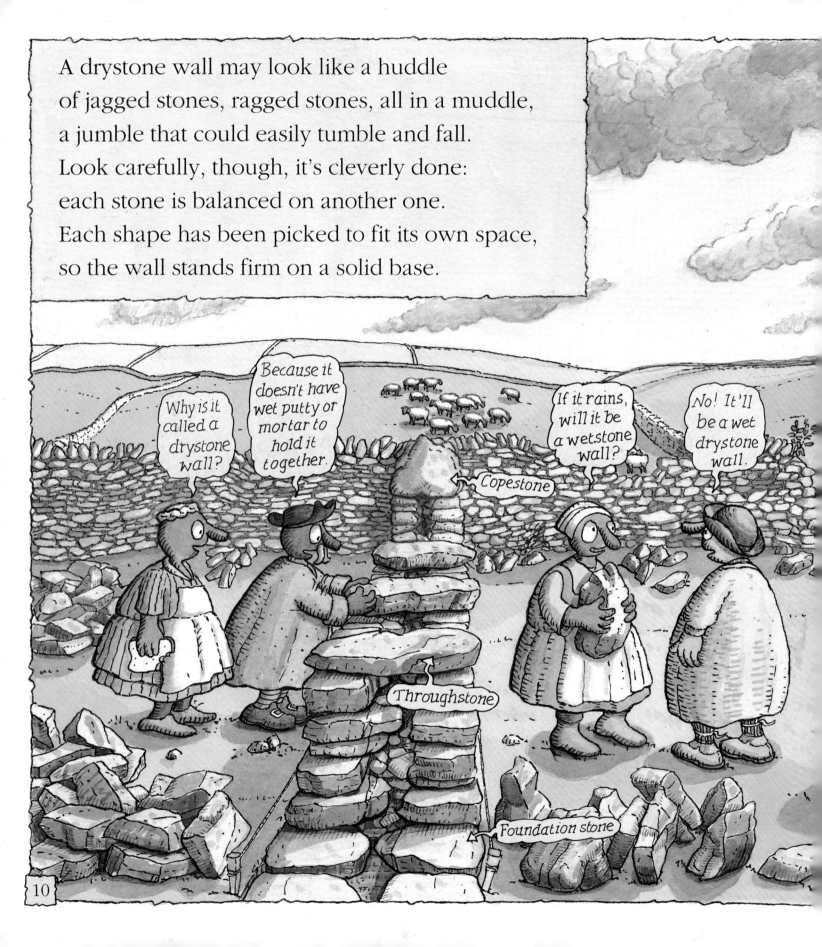

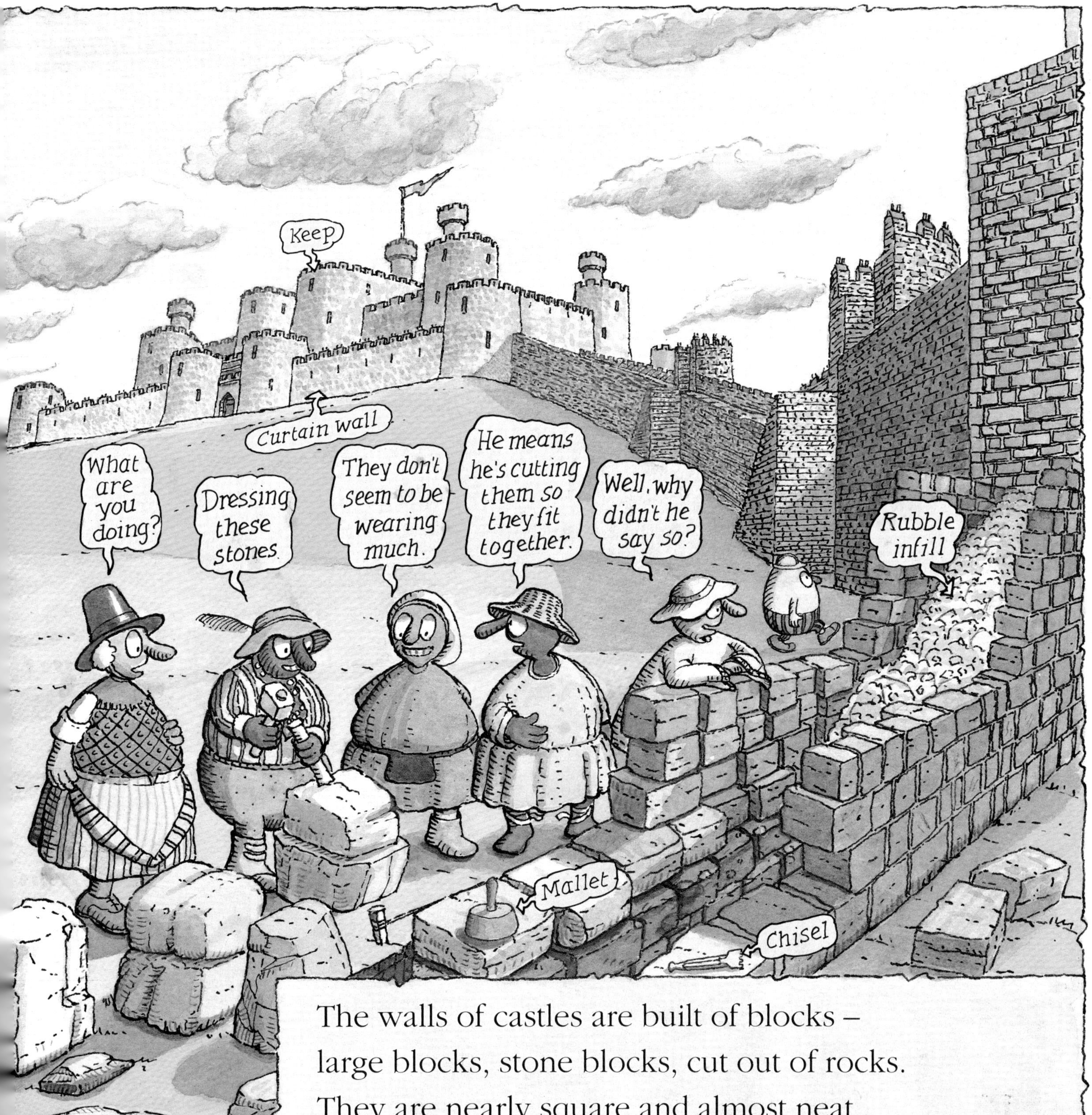
Keep
Curtain wall
What are you doing?
Dressing these stones.
They don't seem to be wearing much.
He means he's cutting them so they fit together.
Well, why didn't he say so?
Rubble infill
Mallet
Chisel

The walls of castles are built of blocks –
large blocks, stone blocks, cut out of rocks.
They are nearly square and almost neat
and mortar joins them where they meet.

We missed a bit right over there!
Cave painting

There are walls made of glass that shine in the sun,
and rubbery walls that are silly – but fun!

There are brick walls and thick walls and walls owned by cats, and deep underground there are cave walls, with bats.

There

are

tall

walls,

high

walls,

climb

up

to

the

sky

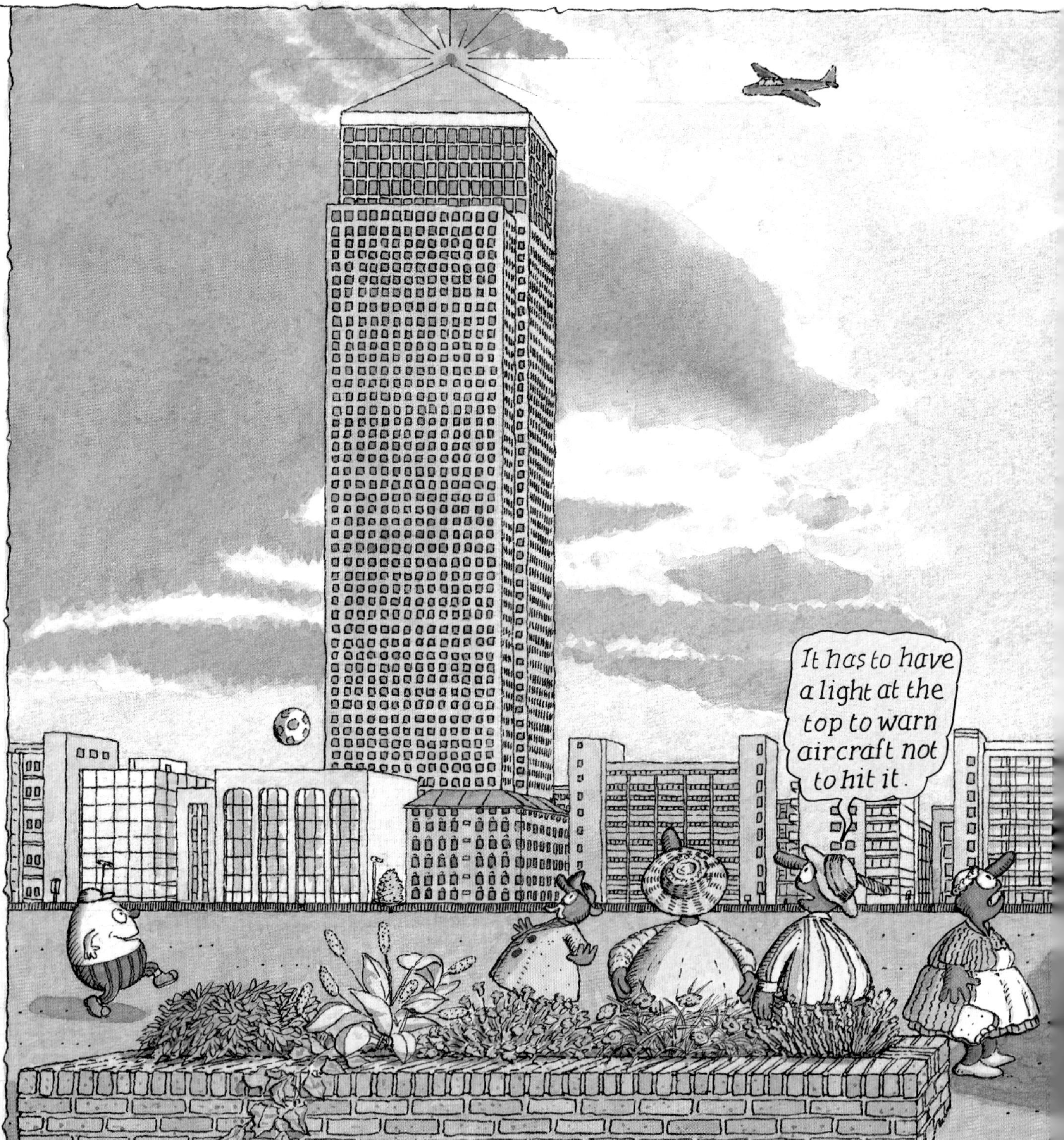
It has to have a light at the top to warn aircraft not to hit it.

walls... and little, low, short walls that creep along the ground.

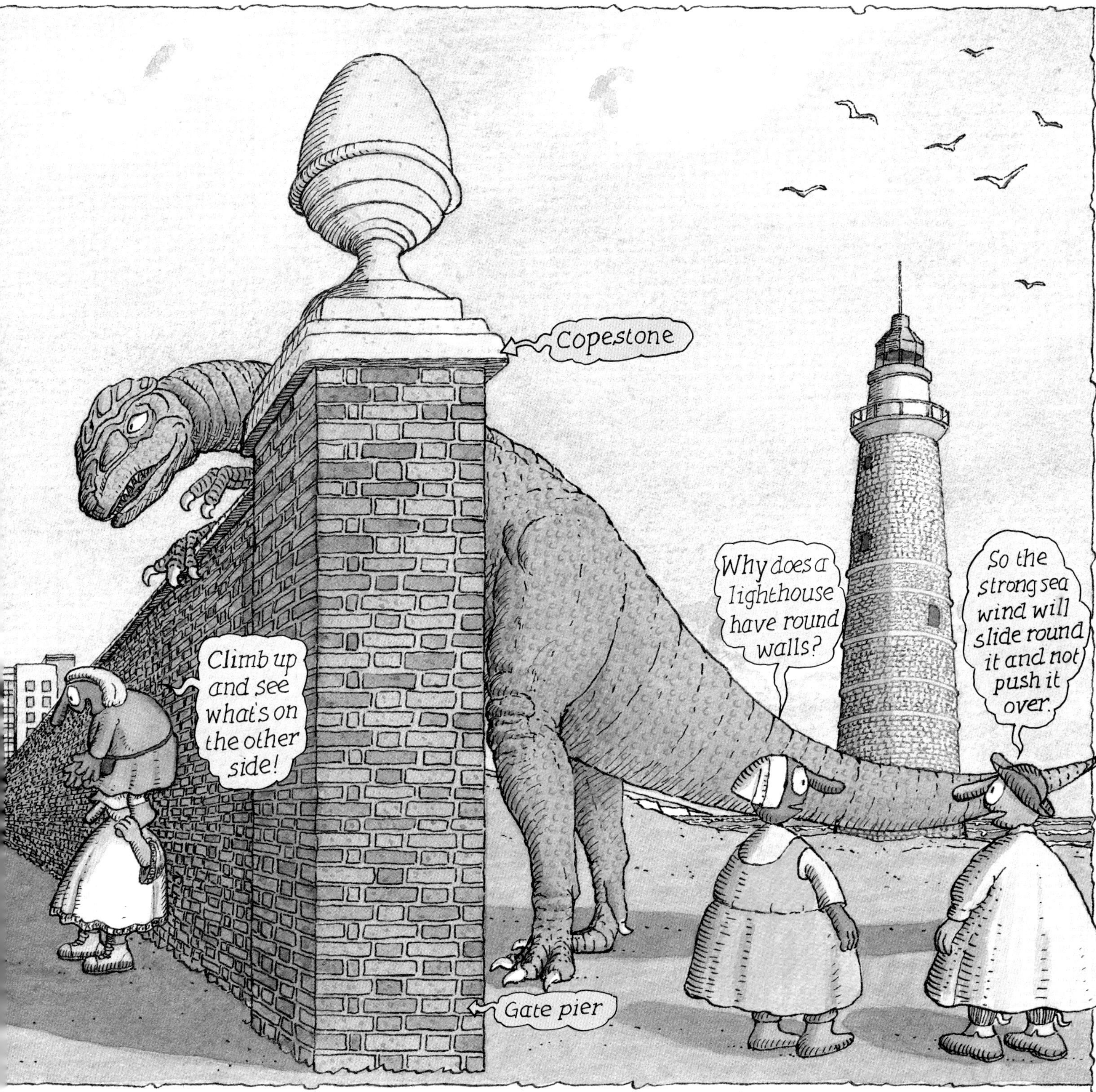
Copestone
Climb up and see what's on the other side!
Why does a lighthouse have round walls?
So the strong sea wind will slide round it and not push it over.
Gate pier

There are big, long, wide walls, we've-got-something-to-hide walls,
and the walls of a lighthouse that have to be round.

There are walls that are horribly fierce,

Everybody GO AWAY!!
PRIVATE KEEP OUT!
NOBODY WELCOME HERE!
NO BALL GAMES
NO FUN

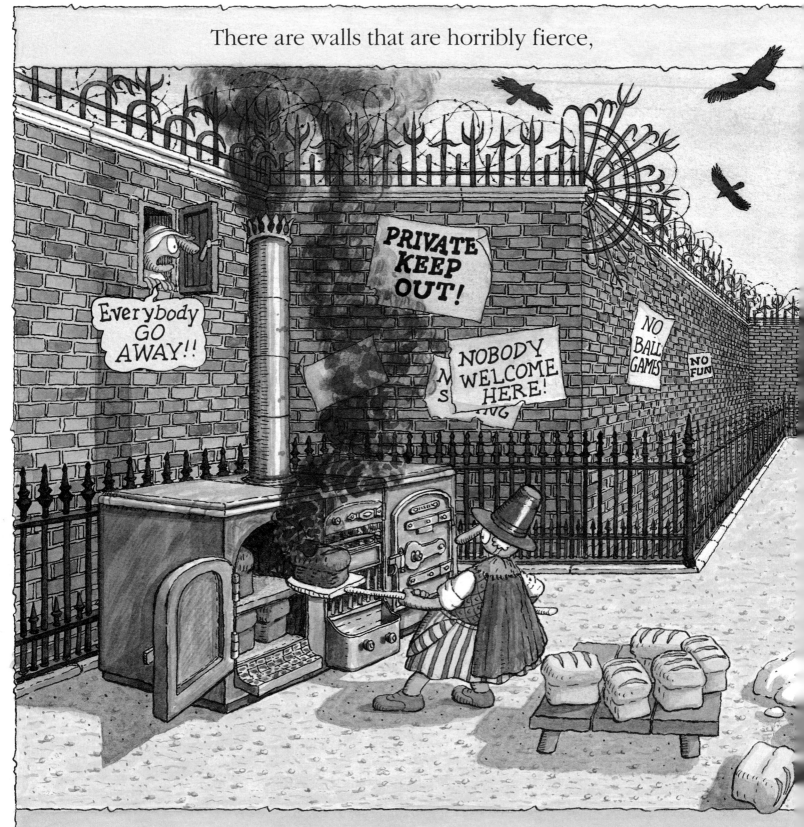

There are walls that are meant to get hot,

and walls that are terribly old.

HATE
HATE
This was built by the Romans 2000 years ago.
Didn't last long, did it?
Ice blocks
If the weather gets warmer, these igloo walls will turn into puddles.

and walls that ought to stay cold.

Some walls are there to shut out invaders
(a safe keeps out robbers, a fort keeps out raiders).

Others are different – they're there to shut in.
(Think of people in prison, or beans in a tin!)

Here is a wall that has to be tough
so it won't collapse when the weather gets rough,

What's this wall for?
It's to stop the sea flooding the town!
Sea wall

and the wind is wild and the waves pound hard
and the stormy seas try to break through its guard.

Here is a wall that is long, strong and round:
it's the wall of a tunnel that runs underground.

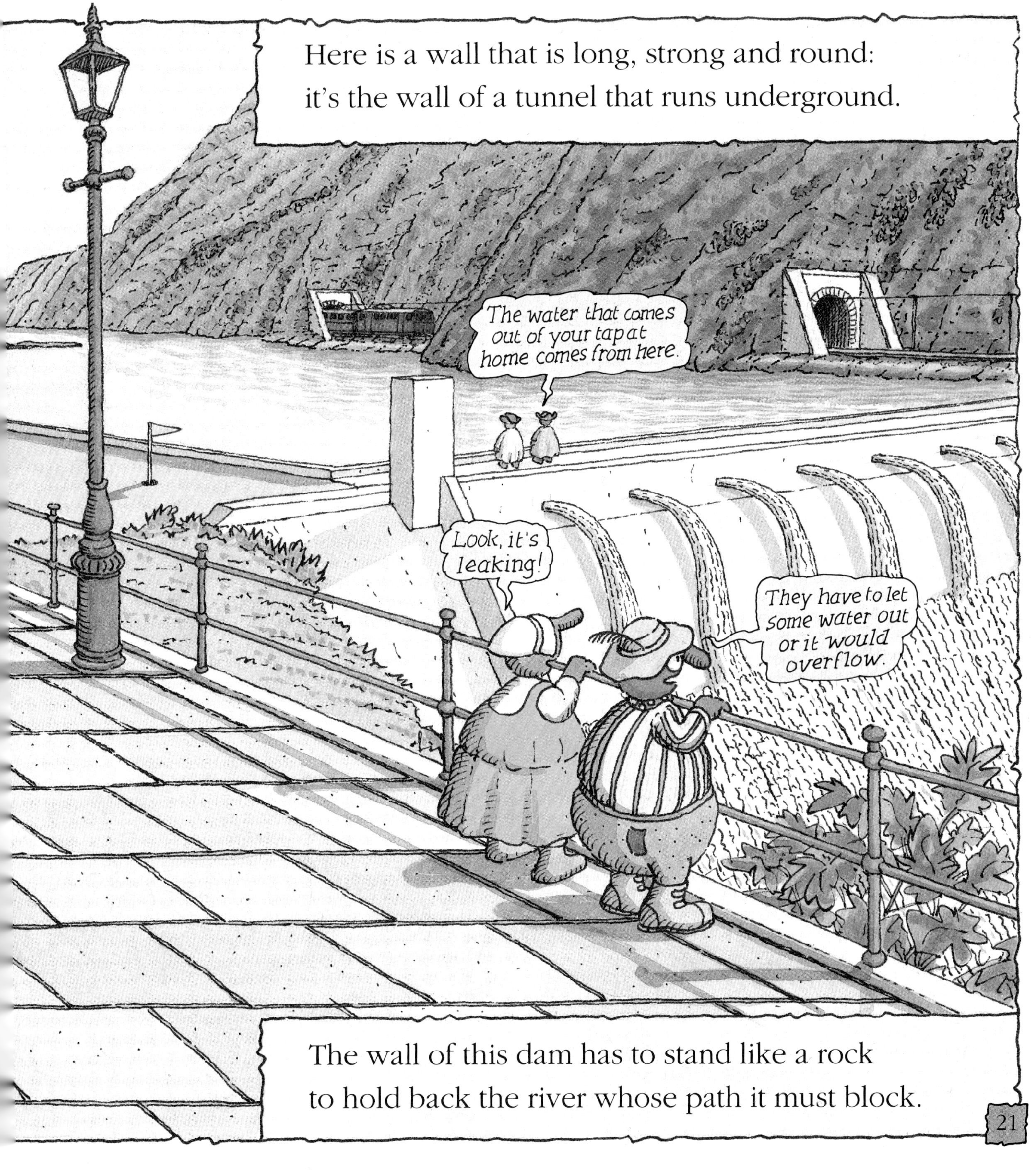
The water that comes out of your tap at home comes from here.
Look, it's leaking!
They have to let some water out or it would overflow.

The wall of this dam has to stand like a rock
to hold back the river whose path it must block.

Cornice
Is this straight?
Yes!
Wallpaper
I had ten green bottles standing on the wall, but one green bottle accidently fell.
So that's why there are nine green bottles standing on the wall.

Most indoor walls are plain and flat,

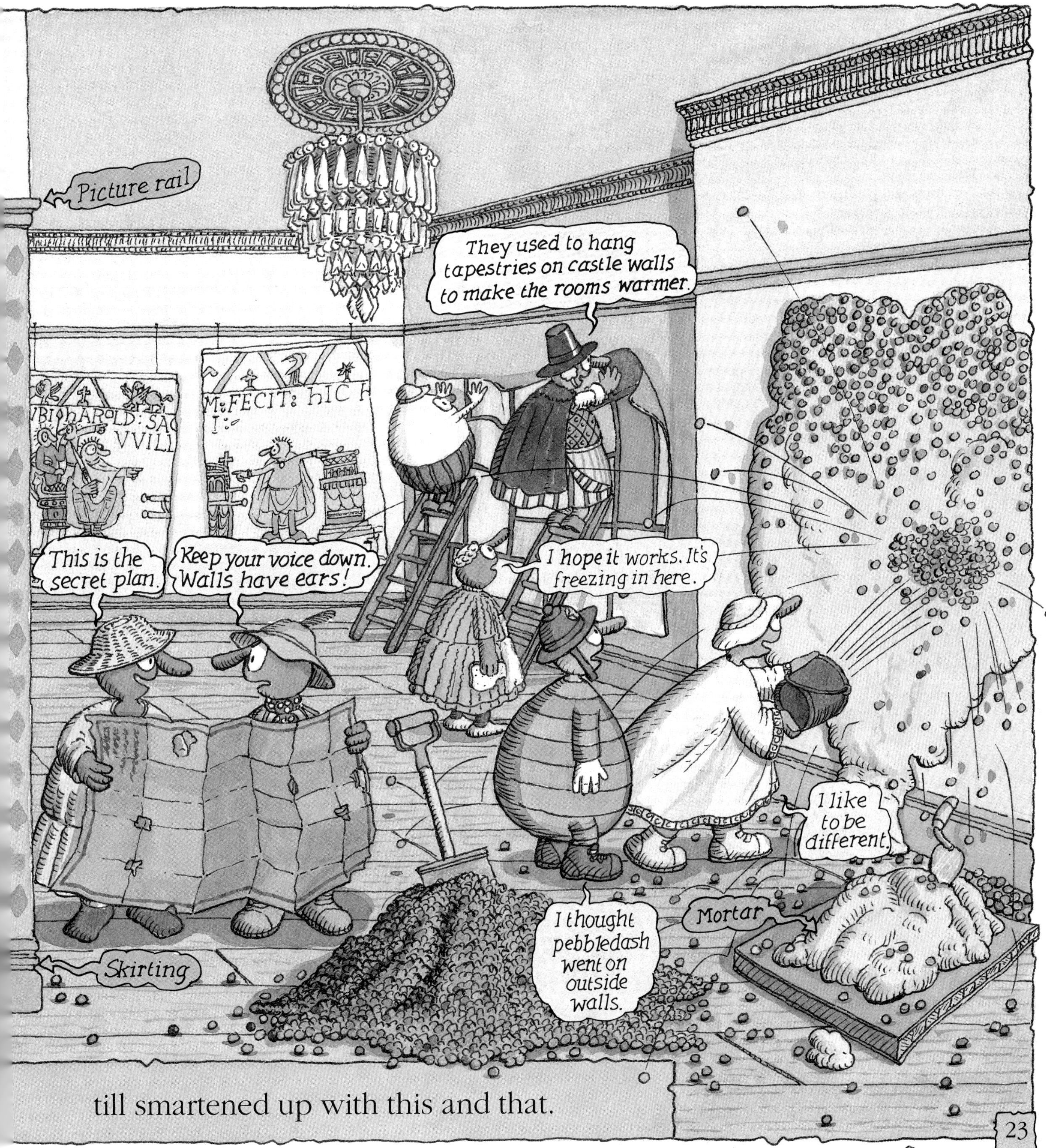
Picture rail
They used to hang tapestries on castle walls to make the rooms warmer.
This is the secret plan.
Keep your voice down. Walls have ears!
I hope it works. It's freezing in here.
I like to be different.
Mortar
I thought pebbledash went on outside walls.
Skirting

till smartened up with this and that.

Moth
Caterpillar
Snail
Humpty Dumpty's sitting on the wall.
If he's not careful, he'll have a great fall.
Centipede

If you sit on a wall you may not be alone.

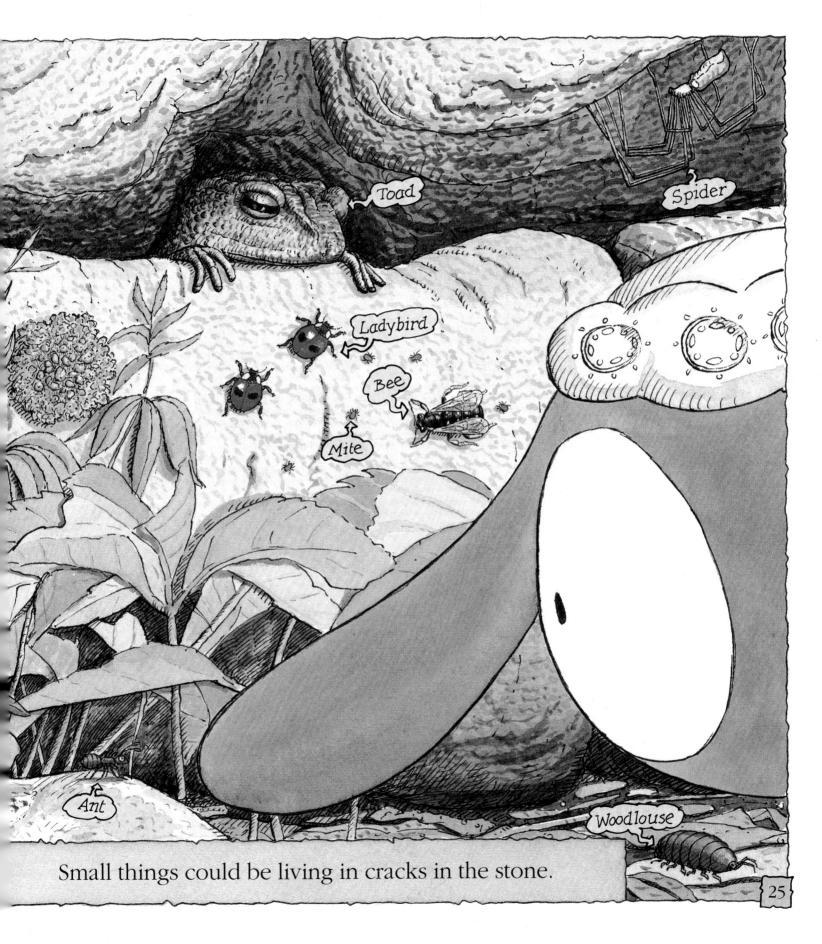

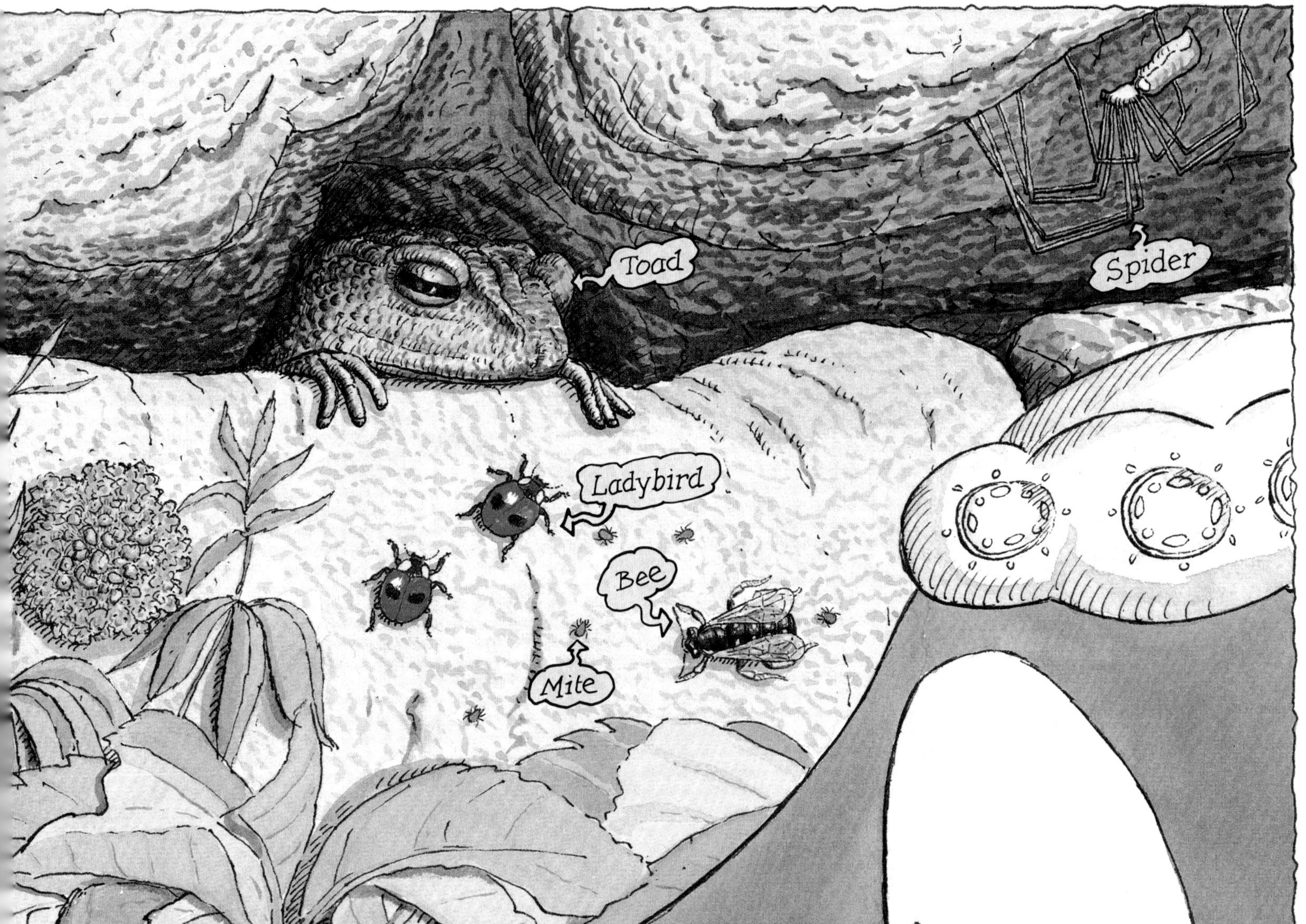

Small things could be living in cracks in the stone.

If you want to climb a mountain wall you will probably need stout boots and crampons and warm clothing and pegs to hammer into narrow cracks and wedges to hammer into wide cracks and a peg hammer to put them in with and an ice axe and a hammer axe (which is a short ice axe) and a strong rope and a hard hat.

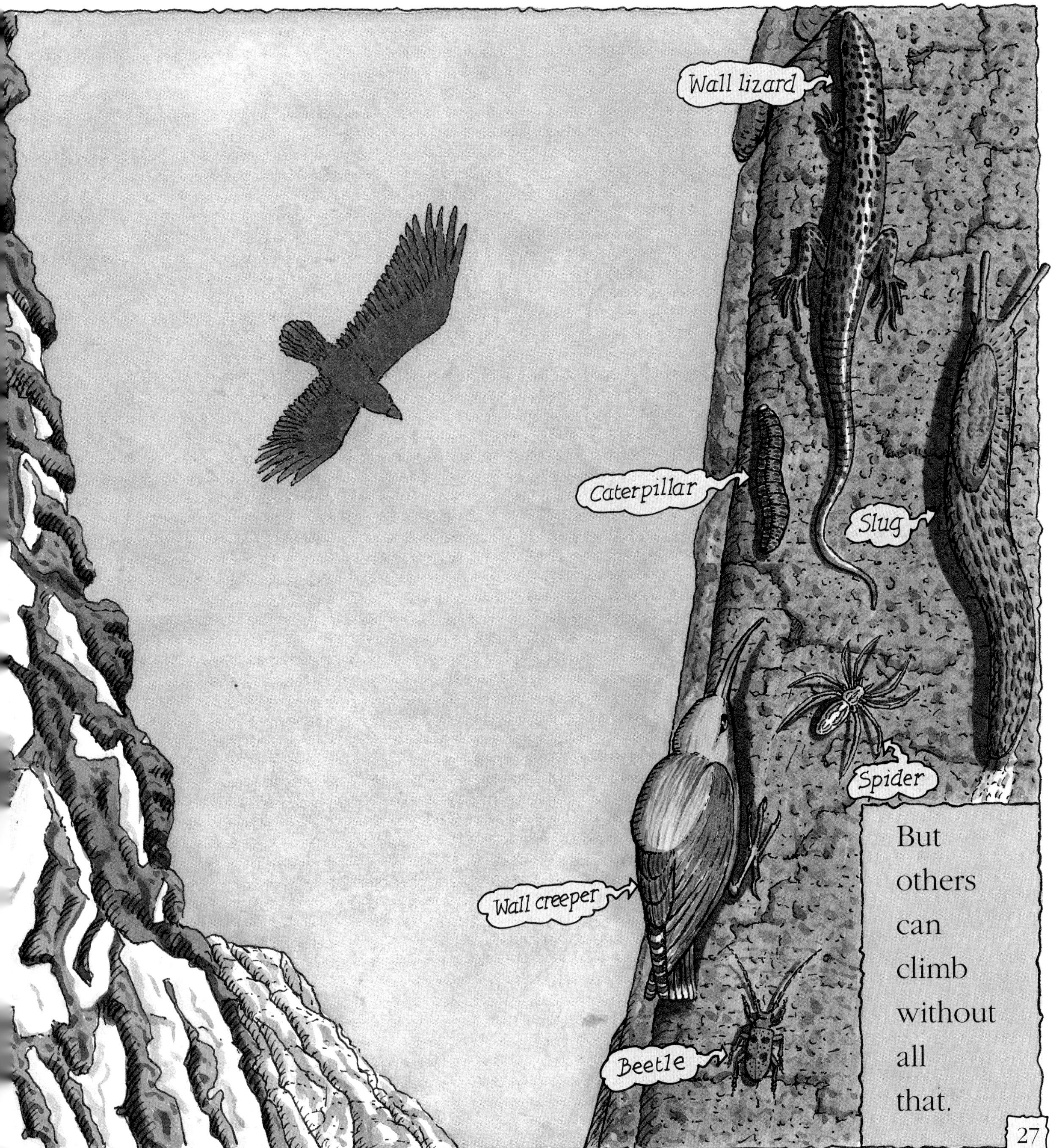

But others can climb without all that.

WHERE ARE YOU?

Where are you? In a room? In a garden? In a car? A bus? A train?
In a field? On a boat? Maybe up in a plane?
In the street? On the beach? In a hot-air balloon?

They say you can see the Great Wall of China from the moon.
Why? How long is it?
2400 kilometres.
Well, I can't see it!
Nor can I!
Perhaps we should have brought a telescope.
I suppose there are no walls on the moon.
What about crater walls?

In a café? In bed? Perhaps on the moon?
Well, wherever you are when you finish this book,
I bet you can see a wall, if you look.

Bevelled bat brick

Dogleg brick

Index

Half round coping brick

Plinth squint brick

Look up the pages to find out about all these walls. Don't forget to look at both kinds of words: this kind and *this kind*.

Decorative brick

Limestone sneck

Bevelled bat brick

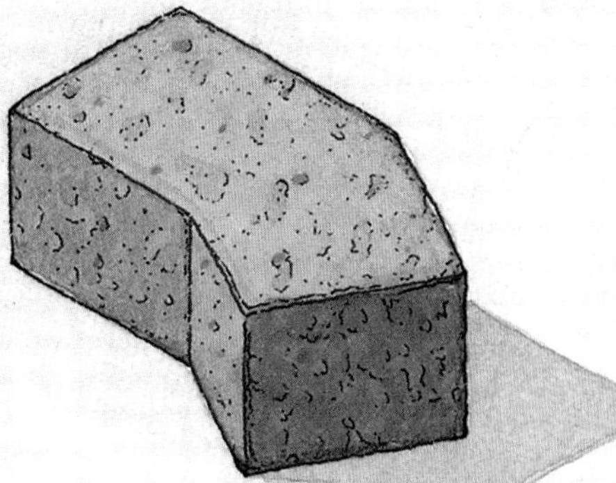
Dogleg brick

A note from the author

Judy Allen got the idea for this book when she was watching a television programme about a wall that divided a country. "I was watching this horrible wall being pulled down," she says, "and after that I was amazed at how many different kinds of wall I could think of without even trying. I decided there was a book in there somewhere!"

Half round coping brick

Plinth squint brick

A note from the illustrator

Alan Baron says, "I once built a wall. It was to be nine inches thick. As the wall grew, it got thicker and thicker. At three feet high the wall was eleven inches thick. I wasn't very good at it. Then I improved. At six feet high the wall was back to nine inches thick. To this day the wall has a great big bulge in the middle. No one knows why. Except me."

Decorative brick

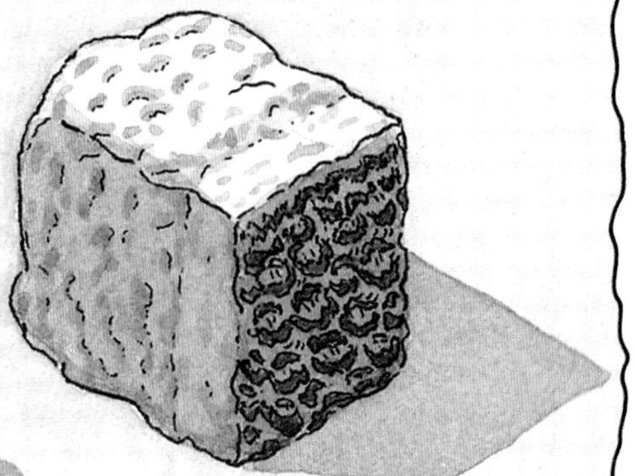
Limestone sneck

NOTES FOR TEACHERS

R E A D A N D W O N D E R

The READ AND WONDER series is an innovative and versatile resource for reading, thinking and discovery. Each book invites children to become excited about a topic, see how varied information books can be, and want to find out more.

Reading aloud The story form makes these books ideal for reading aloud – in their own right or as part of a cross-curricular topic, to a child or to a whole class. After you've introduced children to the books in this way, they can revisit and enjoy them again and again.

Shared reading Big Book editions are available for several titles, so children can read along, discuss the topic, and comment on the different ways information is presented – to wonder together.

Group and guided reading Children need to experience a range of reading materials. Information books like these help develop the skills of reading to learn, as part of learning to read. With the support of a reading group, children can become confident, flexible readers.

Paired reading It's fun to take turns to read the information in the main text or captions. With a partner, children can explore the pages to satisfy their curiosity and build their understanding.

Individual reading These books can be read for interest and pleasure by children at home and in school.

Research Once children have been introduced to these books through reading aloud, they can use them for independent or group research, as part of a curricular topic.

Children's own writing You can offer these books as strong models for children's own information writing. They can record their observations and findings about a topic, make field notes and sketches, and add extra snippets of information for the reader.

Above all, Read and Wonders are to be enjoyed, and encourage children to develop a lasting curiosity about the world they live in.

Sue Ellis, Centre for Language in Primary Education